M000198632

To

Laurie Horne

From

Linda Alxander's
S.S. Class - Cranston
F.W.B. Church

GOD
Comforts
YOU

A Treasury of
GOD'S PROMISES

God Comforts You

A Treasury of God's Promises
© 2009 Ellie Claire Gift & Paper Corp.
www.ellieclaire.com

Compiled by Joanie Garborg
Designed by Jenny Bethke

Scripture references are from the following sources: The Holy Bible, King James Version (KJV). The New King James Version (NKJV). Copyright © 1982 by Thomas Nelson, Inc. Used by permission. The Holy Bible, English Standard Version® (ESV), copyright © 2001 by Crossway Bibles, a publishing ministry of Good News Publishers. Used by permission. All rights reserved. The New American Standard Bible® (NASB), Copyright © 1960, 1962, 1963, 1968, 1971, 1972, 1973, 1975, 1977, 1995 by The Lockman Foundation. Used by permission. The Holy Bible, New International Version®, NIV® Copyright © 1973, 1978, 1984 by International Bible Society. Used by permission of Zondervan. The New Revised Standard Version Bible (NRSV), copyright 1989, 1995, Division of Christian Education of the National Council of the Churches of Christ in the United States of America. Used by permission. The Holy Bible, New Living Translation (NLT), copyright 1996, 2004. Used by permission of Tyndale House Publishers, Inc., Wheaton, Illinois. *The Message*. Copyright © 1993, 1994, 1995, 1996, 2000, 2001, 2002 by Eugene Peterson. Used by permission of NavPress, Colorado Springs, CO. All rights reserved.

ISBN 978-1-935416-23-4

Printed in China

CONTENTS

The God of All Comfort 8
I Will Comfort You 10
He Binds the Brokenhearted 12
Unfailing Love 14
The Lord Sustains Me 16
God With Us 18
Lifter of My Head 20
Steadfast Love and Faithfulness 22
Peace, Perfect Peace 24
God So Loved 26
Trust at All Times 28
Teach Me Your Paths 30
Reassuring Presence 32
He Intercedes for Us 34
In the Day of Trouble 36
The Rising of the Sun 38
His Name Is Near 40
Listen to My Prayer 42
Lavish Love 44
Faith Is... 46
He Cares for You 48
Compassion Over All 50
Light Dawns 52
Wait on the Lord 54
His Ways Are Higher 56
Life God's Way 58
Still the Storms 60
Tested as Gold 62
For He Is Good 64
At Home in His Love 66
Everlasting Arms 68

Unspeakably Precious 70

Strong Support 72

He Knows Your Needs 74

The Shelter of the Most High 76

The Light of His Love 78

Ask, Seek, Knock 80

He Is with Me 82

Yet I Will Praise 84

Multiplied Peace 86

Fresh Hope 88

Gently Led 90

As Good as His Word 92

Made Perfect in Weakness 94

Remember His Love 96

Faithful from Every Angle 98

Deep and Hidden Things 100

Our Great High Priest 102

Near to All Who Call 104

Living Water 106

Guard Your Heart 108

Send Forth Your Light 110

My Help and Shield 112

At Every Moment 114

A Tower of Strength 116

Made Whole 118

His Name and Renown 120

Faithful Promises 122

Showers in Season 124

Be Still and Know 126

Everlasting Love 128

THE GOD
OF ALL COMFORT

Blessed be the God and Father of our Lord Jesus Christ, the Father of mercies and God of all comfort, who comforts us in all our affliction so that we will be able to comfort those who are in any affliction with the comfort with which we ourselves are comforted by God.

2 CORINTHIANS 1:3-4 NASB

The LORD is near to the brokenhearted and saves those who are crushed in spirit.

PSALM 34:18 NASB

I, even I, am he who comforts you.

ISAIAH 51:12 NIV

He heals the brokenhearted and binds up their wounds. He determines the number of the stars; he gives to all of them their names. Great is our Lord, and abundant in power; his understanding is beyond measure.... The Lord takes pleasure in those who fear him, in those who hope in his steadfast love.

PSALM 147:3-5, 11 ESV

Only God can truly comfort;
He comes alongside us and shows us
how deeply and tenderly
He feels for us in our sorrow.

I WILL COMFORT YOU

He is despised and rejected of men; a man of
sorrows, and acquainted with grief:
and we hid as it were our faces from him;
he was despised, and we esteemed him not.
Surely he hath borne our griefs, and carried our
sorrows...and with his stripes we are healed.

ISAIAH 53:3-5 KJV

For the LORD has comforted His people...that all the
ends of the earth may see the salvation of our God.

ISAIAH 52:9-10 NASB

Blessed are they that mourn:
for they shall be comforted.

MATTHEW 5:4 KJV

May our Lord Jesus Christ himself and God
our Father, who loved us and by his grace
gave us eternal comfort and a wonderful hope,
comfort you and strengthen you in
every good thing you do and say.

2 THESSALONIANS 2:16-17 NLT

*When Jesus...confides to us that
He is "acquainted with Grief,"
we listen, for that also is an
Acquaintance of our own.*

— *Emily Dickinson* —

11

HE BINDS
THE BROKENHEARTED

The Spirit of the Sovereign LORD is on me,
because the LORD has anointed me to preach
good news to the poor. He has sent me to bind
up the brokenhearted, to proclaim freedom for
the captives and release from darkness for the
prisoners, to proclaim the year of the LORD's
favor and the day of vengeance of our God, to
comfort all who mourn, and provide for those
who grieve in Zion—to bestow on them a crown
of beauty instead of ashes, the oil of gladness
instead of mourning, and a garment of praise
instead of a spirit of despair.
They will be called oaks of righteousness,
a planting of the LORD for the display
of his splendor.

ISAIAH 61:1-3 NIV

A bruised reed he will not break, and a
dimly burning wick he will not quench;
he will faithfully bring forth justice.

ISAIAH 42:3 NRSV

As for me, I am poor and needy,
but the Lord takes thought for me.

PSALM 40:17 NRSV

*The Lord promises to bind up
the brokenhearted, to give relief and
full deliverance to those whose spirits
have been weighed down.*

— *Charles R. Swindoll* —

13

UNFAILING LOVE

But God, being rich in mercy, because of the great love with which he loved us...raised us up with him and seated us with him in the heavenly places in Christ Jesus, so that in the coming ages he might show the immeasurable riches of his grace in kindness toward us in Christ Jesus.

EPHESIANS 2:4, 6-7 ESV

I will sing of the LORD's unfailing love forever! Young and old will hear of your faithfulness.

PSALM 89:1 NLT

Let them give thanks to the LORD for his unfailing love.

PSALM 107:8-9 NIV

Satisfy us in the morning with your
unfailing love, that we may sing for joy
and be glad all our days.

PSALM 90:14 NIV

For your unfailing love is as high as the
heavens. Your faithfulness reaches to the clouds.
Be exalted, O God, above the highest heavens.
May your glory shine over all the earth.

PSALM 57:10-11 NLT

*Everything God does is love—even
when we do not understand Him.*

— *Basilea Schlink* —

THE LORD SUSTAINS ME

Listen to me...you whom I have upheld since
you were conceived, and have carried since
your birth. Even to your old age and gray hairs
I am he, I am he who will sustain you.
I have made you and I will carry you;
I will sustain you and I will rescue you.

ISAIAH 46:3-4 NIV

But you, O LORD, are a shield about me,
my glory, and the lifter of my head.
I cried aloud to the LORD, and he
answered me from his holy hill....
I lay down and slept; I woke again,
for the LORD sustained me.

PSALM 3:3-5 ESV

Cast your burden on the LORD, and
He shall sustain you; He shall never
permit the righteous to be moved.

PSALM 55:22 NKJV

Restore to me the joy of your salvation and
grant me a willing spirit, to sustain me.

PSALM 51:12 NIV

*God is adequate as our keeper…. Your
faith will not fail while God sustains it;
you are not strong enough to fall away
while God is resolved to hold you.*

— J. I. Packer —

How lovely are Your dwelling places,
O LORD of hosts! My soul longed and even
yearned for the courts of the LORD; my heart
and my flesh sing for joy to the living God....
For a day in Your courts is better
than a thousand outside.

PSALM 84:1-2, 10 NASB

I am with you and will watch over you
wherever you go.

GENESIS 28:15 NIV

And they shall call his name Emmanuel,
which being interpreted is, God with us.

MATTHEW 1:23 KJV

18

You are my hiding place; You preserve me
from trouble; You surround me
with songs of deliverance.

PSALM 32:7 NASB

God is every moment totally aware of each one of us. Totally aware in intense concentration and love.... No one passes through any area of life, happy or tragic, without the attention of God with him.

— *Eugenia Price* —

LIFTER OF MY HEAD

Many are saying to me, "There is no help for you in God." But you, O Lord, are a shield around me, my glory, and the one who lifts up my head. I cry aloud to the Lord, and he answers me from his holy hill.

PSALM 3:2-4 NRSV

Let the beloved of the LORD rest secure in him, for he shields him all day long, and the one the LORD loves rests between his shoulders.

DEUTERONOMY 33:12 NIV

The LORD upholds all who fall, and raises up all who are bowed down.

PSALM 145:14 NKJV

I lift my eyes to you, O God, enthroned in heaven.
We keep looking to the LORD our God for his mercy.

PSALM 123:1-2 NLT

Then the God who lifts up the downcast
lifted our heads and our hearts.

2 CORINTHIANS 7:6 THE MESSAGE

*I lift up mine eyes to the quiet hills,
and my heart to the Father's throne;
in all my ways, to the end of days,
the Lord will preserve His own.*

— *Timothy Dudley-Smith* —

STEADFAST LOVE
AND FAITHFULNESS

The steadfast love of the LORD never ceases;
his mercies never come to an end; they are new
every morning; great is your faithfulness.
"The LORD is my portion," says my soul,
"therefore I will hope in him." The LORD is good
to those who wait for him, to the soul
who seeks him.... Though he cause grief, he will
have compassion according to the abundance
of his steadfast love; for he does not willingly
afflict or grieve the children of men.

LAMENTATIONS 3:22-25, 32-33 ESV

For GOD is sheer beauty, all-generous in love,
loyal always and ever.

PSALM 100:5 THE MESSAGE

O give thanks to the Lord, for he is good, for his steadfast love endures forever.... O give thanks to the Lord of lords, for his steadfast love endures forever; who alone does great wonders, for his steadfast love endures forever.

PSALM 136:1, 3-4 NRSV

Whether we feel strong or weak in our faith, we remember that our assurance is... in the faithfulness of God. We focus on His trustworthiness and especially on His steadfast love.

— Richard J. Foster —

23

PEACE, PERFECT PEACE

I have told you these things, so that in me
you may have peace. In this world
you will have trouble. But take heart!
I have overcome the world.

JOHN 16:33 NIV

Let not your heart be troubled: ye believe in
God, believe also in me. In my Father's house
are many mansions: if it were not so, I would
have told you. I go to prepare a place for you.
And if I go and prepare a place for you, I will
come again, and receive you unto myself; that
where I am, there ye may be also....
I will not leave you comfortless:

I will come to you.... Peace I leave with you,
my peace I give unto you: not as the world
giveth, give I unto you. Let not your heart
be troubled, neither let it be afraid.

JOHN 14:1-3, 18, 27 KJV

*Trials...may come in abundance. But
they cannot penetrate into the sanctuary
of the soul when it is settled in God,
and we may dwell in perfect peace.*

— Hannah Whitall Smith —

25

GOD SO LOVED

For God so loved the world, that he gave his only begotten Son, that whosoever believeth in him should not perish, but have everlasting life. For God sent not his Son into the world to condemn the world; but that the world through him might be saved.

JOHN 3:16-17 KJV

God's love is meteoric, his loyalty astronomic, his purpose titanic, his verdicts oceanic. Yet in his largeness nothing gets lost.

PSALM 36:5-6 THE MESSAGE

May the Lord direct your hearts into the love of God.

2 THESSALONIANS 3:5 NASB

This is My commandment, that you
love one another, just as I have loved you.
Greater love has no one than this, that one
lay down his life for his friends.

JOHN 15:12-13 NASB

You, O God, are both tender and kind,
not easily angered, immense in love,
and you never, never quit.

PSALM 86:15 THE MESSAGE

The love of God is broader
than the measure of our mind
and the heart of the Eternal
is most wonderfully kind.

— *Frederick W. Faber* —

TRUST AT ALL TIMES

My soul finds rest in God alone; my salvation comes from him. He alone is my rock and my salvation; he is my fortress, I will never be shaken.... My salvation and my honor depend on God; he is my mighty rock, my refuge. Trust in him at all times, O people; pour out your hearts to him, for God is our refuge.... One thing God has spoken, two things have I heard: that you, O God, are strong, and that you, O Lord, are loving.

PSALM 62:1-2, 7-8, 11-12 NIV

Trust steadily in God, hope unswervingly, love extravagantly. And the best of the three is love.

1 CORINTHIANS 13:13 THE MESSAGE

Rest in the LORD, and wait patiently for him.

PSALM 37:7 KJV

Trust in the LORD with all your heart, and lean not on your own understanding.

PROVERBS 3:5 NKJV

God may be trusted because He is the True One. He is true, He acts truly, and He speaks truly.... Truthfulness is therefore foundational for His trustworthiness.

— *Os Guinness* —

TEACH ME YOUR PATHS

To You, O LORD, I lift up my soul. O my God,
in You I trust, do not let me be ashamed....
Make me know Your ways, O LORD; teach me
Your paths. Lead me in Your truth and teach
me, for You are the God of my salvation; for
You I wait all the day. Remember, O LORD,
Your compassion and Your lovingkindnesses,
for they have been from of old....
All the paths of the LORD are lovingkindness
and truth to those who keep His covenant and
His testimonies.

PSALM 25:1-2, 4-6, 10 NASB

In all your ways acknowledge Him, and He
shall direct your paths.

PROVERBS 3:6 NKJV

Come, let us go up to the mountain of the LORD,
to the house of the God of Jacob. He will teach
us his ways, so that we may walk in his paths.

ISAIAH 2:3 NIV

Love GOD, your God. Walk in his ways.
Keep his commandments, regulations, and rules
so that you will live, really live, live exuberantly,
blessed by GOD.

DEUTERONOMY 30:16 THE MESSAGE

What we need is not new light,
but new sight; not new paths, but
new strength to walk in the old ones.

REASSURING PRESENCE

Where can I go from your Spirit? Where can
I flee from your presence? If I go up to the
heavens, you are there; if I make my bed in the
depths, you are there. If I rise on the wings of
the dawn, if I settle on the far side of the sea,
even there your hand will guide me, your right
hand will hold me fast.

PSALM 139:7-10 NIV

I look behind me and you're there, then up
ahead and you're there, too—your reassuring
presence, coming and going. This is too much,
too wonderful—I can't take it all in!

PSALM 139:5-6 THE MESSAGE

The LORD your God is with you, he is
mighty to save. He will take great delight
in you, he will quiet you with his love, he will
rejoice over you with singing.

ZEPHANIAH 3:17 NIV

*God is present at every point in space....
We cannot even conceive of a place
where He is not.... People do not know
if God is here. What a difference
it would make if they knew.*

— A. W. Tozer —

HE INTERCEDES FOR US

The Holy Spirit helps us in our weakness.
For example, we don't know what God
wants us to pray for. But the Holy Spirit prays
for us with groanings that cannot be expressed
in words. And the Father who knows all hearts
knows what the Spirit is saying, for the Spirit
pleads for us believers in harmony
with God's own will.

ROMANS 8:26-27 NLT

I will remain in the world no longer, but they
are still in the world, and I am coming to you.
Holy Father, protect them by the
power of your name.

JOHN 17:11 NIV

Jesus...because He continues forever, holds His priesthood permanently. Therefore He is able also to save forever those who draw near to God through Him, since He always lives to make intercession for them.

HEBREWS 7:24-25 NASB

If we knew how to listen, we would hear Him speaking to us.... If we knew how to listen to God, if we knew how to look around us, our whole life would become prayer.

— *Michael Quoist* —

IN THE DAY OF TROUBLE

The LORD is my light and my salvation—whom shall I fear? The LORD is the stronghold of my life—of whom shall I be afraid?...

One thing I ask of the LORD, this is what I seek: that I may dwell in the house of the LORD all the days of my life, to gaze upon the beauty of the LORD and to seek him in his temple.

For in the day of trouble he will keep me safe in his dwelling; he will hide me in the shelter of his tabernacle and set me high upon a rock....

Hear my voice when I call, O LORD; be merciful to me and answer me. My heart says of you, "Seek his face!" Your face, LORD, I will seek.

PSALM 27:1, 4-5, 7-8 NIV

I love those who love me; and those
who diligently seek me will find me.

PROVERBS 8:17 NASB

I will take the load from your shoulders;
I will free your hands from their heavy tasks.
You cried to me in trouble, and I saved you.

PSALM 81:6-7 NLT

Leave for a season the remembrance of
your troubles and dwell on the lovingkindness of God, that you may recover
by gazing on Him.

THE RISING OF THE SUN

Blessed be the name of the LORD from
this time forth and forevermore! From the
rising of the sun to its going down
the LORD's name is to be praised.

PSALM 113:2-3 NKJV

But for you who fear my name, the sun of
righteousness shall rise with healing in its wings.

MALACHI 4:2 ESV

For the Lord God is a sun and shield; the Lord
gives grace and glory; no good thing does He
withhold from those who walk uprightly.

PSALM 84:11 NASB

May they who love you be like the sun
when it rises in its strength.

JUDGES 5:31 NIV

God is sheer mercy and grace; not easily
angered, he's rich in love.... As far as sunrise is
from sunset, he has separated us from our sins.

PSALM 103:8, 12 THE MESSAGE

*O God, Creator of light: at the rising of
Your sun this morning, let the greatest
of all lights, Your love, rise like the sun
within our hearts.*

39

HIS NAME IS NEAR

It is good to give thanks to the LORD and to sing praises to Your name, O Most High; to declare Your lovingkindness in the morning and Your faithfulness by night.

PSALM 92:1-2 NASB

I will give thanks to the LORD with all my heart; I will tell of all Your wonders. I will be glad and exult in You; I will sing praise to Your name, O Most High.

PSALM 9:1-2 NASB

Your wondrous works declare that Your name is near.

PSALM 75:1 NKJV

Our soul waits for the LORD;

he is our help and our shield.

For our heart is glad in him,

because we trust in his holy name.

Let your steadfast love, O LORD, be upon us,

even as we hope in you.

PSALM 33:20-22 ESV

When God has become...our refuge and
our fortress, then we can reach out to
Him in the midst of a broken world and
feel at home while still on the way.

— *Henri J. M. Nouwen* —

LISTEN TO MY PRAYER

Our Father which art in heaven, Hallowed be
thy name. Thy kingdom come. Thy will
be done in earth, as it is in heaven. Give us
this day our daily bread. And forgive us
our debts, as we forgive our debtors. And lead
us not into temptation, but deliver us from evil:
For thine is the kingdom, and the power,
and the glory, for ever. Amen.

MATTHEW 6:9-13 KJV

I love the LORD because he hears my voice and
my prayer for mercy. Because he bends down to
listen, I will pray as long as I have breath!

PSALM 116:1-2 NLT

I call on you, O God, for you will answer me;

give ear to me and hear my prayer.

PSALM 17:6 NIV

Evening, and morning, and at noon, will I pray,

and cry aloud: and he shall hear my voice.

PSALM 55:17 KJV

God listens in compassion and love, just like we do when our children come to us. He delights in our presence.

— Richard J. Foster —

LAVISH LOVE

I lavish unfailing love for
a thousand generations on those who love me
and obey my commands.

EXODUS 20:6 NLT

I pray that out of his glorious riches he may
strengthen you with power through his Spirit
in your inner being, so that Christ may dwell in
your hearts through faith. And I pray that you,
being rooted and established in love, may have
power, together with all the saints, to grasp how
wide and long and high and deep is the love
of Christ, and to know this love that surpasses
knowledge—that you may be filled to the
measure of all the fullness of God.

Now to him who is able to do immeasurably more than all we ask or imagine, according to his power that is at work within us, to him be glory in the church and in Christ Jesus throughout all generations, for ever and ever! Amen.

EPHESIANS 3:16-21 NIV

O the deep, deep love of Jesus—
Vast, unmeasured, boundless, free!
Rolling as a mighty ocean
In its fullness over me.

— *S. Trevor Francis* —

45

FAITH IS...

Now faith is being sure of what we hope for and certain of what we do not see.... By faith we understand that the universe was formed at God's command, so that what is seen was not made out of what was visible....

And without faith it is impossible to please God, because anyone who comes to him must believe that he exists and that he rewards those who earnestly seek him.

HEBREWS 11:1, 3, 6 NIV

So we fix our eyes not on what is seen, but on what is unseen. For what is seen is temporary, but what is unseen is eternal.

2 CORINTHIANS 4:18 NIV

For in the gospel a righteousness from God
is revealed, a righteousness that is by faith
from first to last, just as it is written:
"The righteous will live by faith."

ROMANS 1:17 NIV

Faith, as the Bible defines it, is present-
tense action. Faith means being sure of
what we hope for...now. It means knowing
something is real, this moment, all around
you, even when you don't see it.

— *Joni Eareckson Tada* —

HE CARES FOR YOU

I am the good shepherd. I know my own and
my own know me, just as the Father knows me
and I know the Father; and I lay down
my life for the sheep.

JOHN 10:14-15 ESV

Casting all your care upon him;
for he careth for you.

1 PETER 5:7 KJV

The LORD is good, a refuge in times of trouble.
He cares for those who trust in him.

NAHUM 1:7 NIV

Love GOD, all you saints; GOD takes care of all
who stay close to him.

PSALM 31:23 THE MESSAGE

God remembered us when we were down,
His love never quits....
Takes care of everyone in time of need.
His love never quits.

PSALM 136:23, 25 THE MESSAGE

God...says, "I'll take the burden—don't
give it a thought—leave it to Me."
God is keenly aware that we are
dependent upon Him for life's necessities.

— *Billy Graham* —

49

COMPASSION OVER ALL

The Lord is gracious and merciful,
slow to anger and abounding in steadfast love.
The Lord is good to all, and his compassion is
over all that he has made.... The Lord is faithful
in all his words, and gracious in all his deeds.

PSALM 145:8-9, 13 NRSV

The God who made the world and everything in
it is the Lord of heaven and earth.... He himself
gives all men life and breath and everything
else.... God did this so that men would seek him
and perhaps reach out for him and find him,
though he is not far from each one of us. "For in
him we live and move and have our being."

ACTS 17:24-25, 27-28 NIV

The heavens are yours, and the earth is yours;

everything in the world is yours—

you created it all.

PSALM 89:11 NLT

You keep track of all my sorrows. You have

collected all my tears in your bottle. You have

recorded each one in your book.

PSALM 56:8 NLT

The loving God we serve has

immeasurable compassion and tenderness

toward each of us throughout our lives.

— *James Dobson* —

LIGHT DAWNS

Light arises in the darkness for the upright;
He is gracious and compassionate and righteous.

PSALM 112:4 NASB

It is you who light my lamp; the Lord, my God,
lights up my darkness.

PSALM 18:28 NRSV

Weeping may remain for a night, but rejoicing
comes in the morning.

PSALM 30:5 NIV

The LORD is righteous...He will do no injustice.
Every morning He brings His justice to light;
He does not fail.

ZEPHANIAH 3:5 NASB

The sun will no more be your light by day, nor will the brightness of the moon shine on you, for the LORD will be your everlasting light, and your God will be your glory. Your sun will never set again, and your moon will wane no more; the LORD will be your everlasting light, and your days of sorrow will end.

ISAIAH 60:19-20 NIV

We do not know how this is true—
where would faith be if we did?—but we
do know that all things that happen are
full of shining seed. Light is sown
for us—not darkness.

WAIT ON THE LORD

Why do you say..."My way is hidden from the
LORD, and my just claim is passed over
by my God"? Have you not known?
Have you not heard? The everlasting God,
the LORD, the Creator of the ends of the earth,
neither faints nor is weary. His understanding is
unsearchable. He gives power to the weak, and
to those who have no might
He increases strength.

Even the youths shall faint and be weary, and
the young men shall utterly fall, but those who
wait on the LORD shall renew their strength;
they shall mount up with wings like eagles,
they shall run and not be weary,
they shall walk and not faint.

ISAIAH 40:27-31 NKJV

I wait for God as long as he remains in hiding,
while I wait and hope for him. I stand
my ground and hope.

ISAIAH 8:17 THE MESSAGE

For Your salvation I wait, O LORD.

GENESIS 49:18 NASB

There is a place of comfort sweet
Near to the heart of God....
Hold us who wait before Thee
Near to the heart of God.

— Cleland B. McAfee —

HIS WAYS ARE HIGHER

O the depth of the riches both of the wisdom
and knowledge of God! how unsearchable are
his judgments, and his ways past finding out!
For who hath known the mind of the Lord?
or who hath been his counsellor?

ROMANS 11:33-34 KJV

For my thoughts are not your thoughts, neither
are your ways my ways, saith the LORD. For as
the heavens are higher than the earth, so are my
ways higher than your ways, and my thoughts
than your thoughts.

ISAIAH 55:8-9 KJV

He is the Rock, his works are perfect, and all
his ways are just. A faithful God who does
no wrong, upright and just is he.

DEUTERONOMY 32:4 NIV

If you are pleased with me, teach me your ways
so I may know you and continue to
find favor with you.

EXODUS 33:13 NIV

*In both simple and eloquent ways,
our infinite God personally reveals
glimpses of Himself in the finite.*

What happens when we live God's way? He brings gifts into our lives, much the same way that fruit appears in an orchard—things like affection for others, exuberance about life, serenity. We develop a willingness to stick with things, a sense of compassion in the heart, and a conviction that a basic holiness permeates things and people.

GALATIANS 5:22-23 THE MESSAGE

Clothe yourselves with compassion, kindness, humility, gentleness and patience. Bear with each other and forgive whatever grievances you may have against one another. Forgive as the Lord forgave you. And over all these virtues put on love, which binds them all together in perfect unity.

COLOSSIANS 3:12-14 NIV

Whatsoever things are true, whatsoever things are honest, whatsoever things are just, whatsoever things are pure, whatsoever things are lovely, whatsoever things are of good report; if there be any virtue, and if there be any praise, think on these things.

PHILIPPIANS 4:8 KJV

The fountain of beauty is the heart, and every generous thought illustrates the walls of your chamber.

— *Francis Quarles* —

STILL THE STORMS

He rescues you from hidden traps, shields you from deadly hazards. His huge outstretched arms protect you—under them you're perfectly safe; his arms fend off all harm.... "If you'll hold on to me for dear life," says GOD, "I'll get you out of any trouble. I'll give you the best of care if you'll only get to know and trust me. Call me and I'll answer, be at your side in bad times."

PSALM 91:3-4, 14-15 THE MESSAGE

For you are God, my only safe haven...
Why am I discouraged? Why is my heart so sad?
I will put my hope in God!

PSALM 43:2, 5 NLT

Then they cried out to the LORD in their trouble,
and he brought them out of their distress.
He stilled the storm to a whisper; the waves of
the sea were hushed. They were glad when it grew
calm, and he guided them to their desired haven.

PSALM 107:28-30 NIV

Calm me, O Lord, as you stilled the storm,
Still me, O Lord, keep me from harm.
Let all the tumult within me cease,
Enfold me, Lord, in your peace.

— *Celtic Traditional* —

TESTED AS GOLD

All praise to God, the Father of our Lord
Jesus Christ. It is by his great mercy that we
have been born again, because God raised
Jesus Christ from the dead. Now we live with
great expectation.... So be truly glad. There is
wonderful joy ahead, even though you have to
endure many trials for a little while.... These
trials will show that your faith is genuine.

It is being tested as fire tests and purifies gold—
though your faith is far more precious than
mere gold. So when your faith remains strong
through many trials, it will bring you much
praise and glory and honor on the day when
Jesus Christ is revealed.

1 PETER 1:3, 6-7 NLT

But He knows the way I take; when He has
tried me, I shall come forth as gold.

JOB 23:10 NASB

I will refine them like silver
and test them like gold.
They will call on my name
and I will answer them.

ZECHARIAH 13:9 NIV

The dark threads are as needful
In the Weaver's skillful hand
As the threads of gold and silver
In the pattern He has planned.

FOR HE IS GOOD

I would have despaired unless I had believed
that I would see the goodness of the LORD
in the land of the living. Wait for the LORD;
be strong and let your heart take courage;
yes, wait for the LORD.

PSALM 27:13-14 NASB

Oh give thanks to the LORD, for he is good;
for his steadfast love endures forever!

1 CHRONICLES 16:34 ESV

He loveth righteousness and judgment:
the earth is full of the goodness of the LORD.

PSALM 33:5 KJV

Do not let the floodwaters engulf me or the
depths swallow me up or the pit close its
mouth over me. Answer me, O Lord, out of the
goodness of your love; in your great mercy turn
to me. Do not hide your face from your servant;
answer me quickly, for I am in trouble.
Come near and rescue me.

PSALM 69:15-18 NIV

*The joyful birds prolong the strain,
their song with every spring renewed;
the air we breathe, and falling rain,
each softly whispers: God is good.*

— *John Hampden Gurney* —

AT HOME IN HIS LOVE

Lord, You have been our dwelling place
in all generations.... Even from everlasting
to everlasting, You are God.

PSALM 90:1-2 NASB

Make your home in me just as I do in you.
In the same way that a branch can't
bear grapes by itself but only by being
joined to the vine, you can't bear fruit
unless you are joined with me.
I am the Vine, you are the branches.
When you're joined with me and I with you,
the relation intimate and organic,
the harvest is sure to be abundant.
Separated, you can't produce a thing....

But if you make yourselves at home with me
and my words are at home in you,
you can be sure that whatever you ask
will be listened to and acted upon....
I've loved you the way my Father has loved me.
Make yourselves at home in my love.

JOHN 15:4-9 THE MESSAGE

God is always present in the temple of
your heart...His home. And when you
come in to meet Him there, you find that
it is the one place of deep comfort and
satisfaction where every longing is met.

EVERLASTING ARMS

Ah, Lord GOD! It is you who have made
the heavens and the earth by your great power
and by your outstretched arm!
Nothing is too hard for you.

JEREMIAH 32:17 ESV

"So do not fear, for I am with you; do not
be dismayed, for I am your God. I will
strengthen you and help you; I will uphold you
with my righteous right hand.... For I am the
LORD, your God, who takes hold of your right
hand and says to you, Do not fear; I will help
you. Do not be afraid...for I myself will help
you," declares the LORD, your Redeemer,
the Holy One of Israel.

ISAIAH 41:10, 13-14 NIV

Behold, I have inscribed you
on the palms of My hands.

ISAIAH 49:16 NASB

The eternal God is your refuge, and underneath
are the everlasting arms.

DEUTERONOMY 33:27 NIV

*The everlasting arms are beneath us....
This is God's promise; this is how good
He is. And our self-distrust...must not
cloud the joy with which we lean on our
faithful covenant God.*

— J. I. Packer —

UNSPEAKABLY PRECIOUS

Don't be afraid, I've redeemed you. I've called your name. You're mine. When you're in over your head, I'll be there with you. When you're in rough waters, you will not go down. When you're between a rock and a hard place, it won't be a dead end—because I am God, your personal God, The Holy of Israel, your Savior. I paid a huge price for you...! *That's* how much you mean to me! *That's* how much I love you!

ISAIAH 43:1-4 THE MESSAGE

For you know that it was not with perishable things such as silver or gold that you were redeemed...but with the precious blood of Christ, a lamb without blemish or defect.

1 PETER 1:18-19 NIV

Do you not know that your body is a temple
of the Holy Spirit within you, whom you have
from God? You are not your own, for you were
bought with a price. So glorify God in your body.

1 CORINTHIANS 6:19-20 ESV

*You are in the Beloved...
therefore infinitely dear to the Father,
unspeakably precious to Him. You are
never, not for one second, alone.*

— *Norman F. Dowty* —

STRONG SUPPORT

For the eyes of the LORD move to and fro
throughout the earth that He may strongly
support those whose heart is completely His.

2 CHRONICLES 16:9 NASB

Do not be afraid.... For the LORD your God will
personally go ahead of you. He will neither fail
you nor abandon you.

DEUTERONOMY 31:6 NLT

Be strong and courageous! Do not tremble or
be dismayed, for the LORD your God is with you
wherever you go.

JOSHUA 1:9 NASB

For he hath said, I will never leave thee,
nor forsake thee. So that we may boldly say,
The Lord is my helper, and I will not fear.

HEBREWS 13:5-6 KJV

If God be for us, who can be against us?

ROMANS 8:31 KJV

Let us wait upon God's strengthening aid.... Let us trust in Him.... What we ourselves cannot bear let us bear with the help of Christ. For He is all-powerful.

— Boniface —

HE KNOWS YOUR NEEDS

Look at the birds of the air; they do not sow
or reap or store away in barns, and yet your
heavenly Father feeds them. Are you not much
more valuable than they? Who of you by
worrying can add a single hour to his life?

And why do you worry about clothes?
See how the lilies of the field grow. They do
not labor or spin. Yet I tell you that not even
Solomon in all his splendor was dressed like one
of these. If that is how God clothes the grass
of the field, which is here today and tomorrow
is thrown into the fire, will he not much more
clothe you, O you of little faith?

So do not worry, saying, "What shall we eat?"
or "What shall we drink?" or
"What shall we wear?"

For...your heavenly Father knows that
you need them. But seek first his kingdom
and his righteousness, and all these things
will be given to you as well.

MATTHEW 6:26-33 NIV

Day by day the LORD takes care of the innocent,
and they will receive an inheritance that lasts forever.

PSALM 37:18 NLT

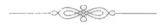

*Trust the past to the mercy of God,
the present to His love, and
the future to His Providence.*

— Augustine —

THE SHELTER
OF THE MOST HIGH

Be merciful to me, O God, be merciful to me, for in you my soul takes refuge; in the shadow of your wings I will take refuge, till the storms of destruction pass by. I cry out to God Most High, to God who fulfills his purpose for me. He will send from heaven and save me.... God will send out his steadfast love and his faithfulness!

PSALM 57:1-3 ESV

He who dwells in the shelter of the Most High will abide in the shadow of the Almighty. I will say to the LORD, "My refuge and my fortress, My God, in whom I trust!"

PSALM 91:1-2 NASB

Blessed be the LORD, my rock...he is my
steadfast love and my fortress, my stronghold
and my deliverer, my shield and he in whom
I take refuge.

PSALM 144:1-2 ESV

The LORD is good, a refuge in times of trouble.
He cares for those who trust in him.

NAHUM 1:7 NIV

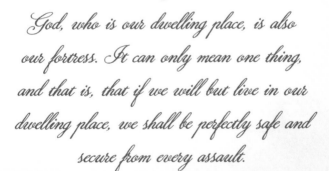

*God, who is our dwelling place, is also
our fortress. It can only mean one thing,
and that is, that if we will but live in our
dwelling place, we shall be perfectly safe and
secure from every assault.*

— *Hannah Whitall Smith* —

THE LIGHT OF HIS LOVE

Your steadfast love, O LORD, extends to the
heavens, your faithfulness to the clouds.
Your righteousness is like the mountains of
God; your judgments are like the great deep;
man and beast you save, O LORD.
How precious is your steadfast love, O God!
The children of mankind take refuge in the
shadow of your wings. They feast on the
abundance of your house, and you give them
drink from the river of your delights.
For with you is the fountain of life;
in your light do we see light.

PSALM 36:5-9 ESV

The sun will no more be your light by day,
nor will the brightness of the moon shine on
you, for the LORD will be your everlasting light,
and your God will be your glory. Your sun will
never set again, and your moon will wane no
more; the LORD will be your everlasting light,
and your days of sorrow will end.

ISAIAH 60:19-20 NIV

It is only when Christ dwells within our
hearts, radiating the pure light of His love
through our humanity that we discover who
we are and what we were intended to be.

ASK, SEEK, KNOCK

Ask, and it will be given to you; seek, and
you will find; knock, and it will be opened to
you. For everyone who asks, receives; and he
who seeks, finds; and to him who knocks,
it will be opened.

LUKE 11:9-10 NASB

And ye shall seek me, and find me,
when ye shall search for me with all your heart.
And I will be found of you, saith the LORD.

JEREMIAH 29:13-14 KJV

Draw near to God and He will draw near to you.

JAMES 4:8 NASB

Seek the LORD your God, and you will find Him
if you seek Him with all your heart and
with all your soul.

DEUTERONOMY 4:29 NKJV

I am standing at the door, knocking; if you hear
my voice and open the door, I will come in to
you and eat with you, and you with me.

REVELATION 3:20 NRSV

They who seek the throne of grace
find that throne in every place;
If we live a life of prayer,
God is present everywhere.

— *Oliver Holden* —

HE IS WITH ME

Yet I am always with you; you hold me by my
right hand. You guide me with your counsel,
and afterward you will take me into glory.
Whom have I in heaven but you? And earth has
nothing I desire besides you. My flesh and my
heart may fail, but God is the strength of my
heart and my portion forever.... As for me, it is
good to be near God. I have made the
Sovereign LORD my refuge.

PSALM 73:23-26, 28 NIV

And the God of love and peace
shall be with you.

2 CORINTHIANS 13:11 KJV

Let all who take refuge in you be glad;
let them ever sing for joy. Spread your
protection over them, that those who love your
name may rejoice in you. For surely, O LORD,
you bless the righteous; you surround them with
your favor as with a shield.

PSALM 5:11-12 NIV

*When I walk by the wayside, He is
along with me.... Amid all my forgetfulness
of Him, He never forgets me.*

— *Thomas Chalmers* —

YET I WILL PRAISE

Even though the fig trees have no blossoms, and
there are no grapes on the vines; even though
the olive crop fails, and the fields lie empty and
barren; even though the flocks die in the fields,
and the cattle barns are empty, yet I will rejoice
in the LORD! I will be joyful in the God of my
salvation! The Sovereign LORD is my strength!

HABAKKUK 3:17-19 NLT

Yet the LORD longs to be gracious to you;
    he rises to show you compassion.
For the LORD is a God of justice.
Blessed are all who wait for him!

ISAIAH 30:18 NIV

But I will hope continually and will
praise you yet more and more.

PSALM 71:14 ESV

Why are you downcast, O my soul? Why so
disturbed within me? Put your hope in God, for
I will yet praise him, my Savior and my God.

PSALM 42:11 NIV

*Trials have no value or intrinsic meaning
in themselves. It's the way we respond to
those trials that makes all the difference.*

— *Joni Eareckson Tada* —

MULTIPLIED PEACE

Don't worry about anything; instead, pray about everything. Tell God what you need, and thank him for all he has done. Then you will experience God's peace, which exceeds anything we can understand. His peace will guard your hearts and minds as you live in Christ Jesus.

PHILIPPIANS 4:6-7 NLT

I will lie down and sleep in peace, for you alone, O LORD, make me dwell in safety.

PSALM 4:8 NIV

The LORD will give strength to His people; the LORD will bless His people with peace.

PSALM 29:11 NKJV

Now the God of peace…make you perfect in
every good work to do his will, working in you
that which is wellpleasing in his sight,
through Jesus Christ; to whom be glory
for ever and ever. Amen.

HEBREWS 13:20-21 KJV

May mercy and peace and love
be multiplied to you.

JUDE 1:2 NASB

God cannot give us a happiness and peace
apart from Himself, because it is not there.
There is no such thing.

— C. S. Lewis —

FRESH HOPE

Why are you in despair, O my soul? And why
have you become disturbed within me?
Hope in God, for I shall again praise Him for
the help of His presence. O my God, my soul is
in despair within me; therefore I remember You.

PSALM 42:5-6 NASB

GOD…rekindles burned-out lives with
fresh hope, restoring dignity and respect to
their lives—a place in the sun! For the very
structures of earth are GOD's; he has laid out his
operations on a firm foundation.

1 SAMUEL 2:7-8 THE MESSAGE

We know that suffering produces perseverance;
perseverance, character; and character, hope.
And hope does not disappoint us, because God
has poured out his love into our hearts by the
Holy Spirit, whom he has given us.

ROMANS 5:3-5 NIV

I place no hope in my strength...but all my
confidence is in God my protector,
who never abandons those who have put
all their hope and thought in Him.

— François Rabelais —

GENTLY LED

He shall feed his flock like a shepherd: he shall
gather the lambs with his arm, and carry them
in his bosom, and shall gently lead those
that are with young.

ISAIAH 40:11 KJV

The LORD is my shepherd; I shall not want.
He makes me to lie down in green pastures;
He leads me beside the still waters.
He restores my soul; He leads me in the paths
of righteousness for His name's sake.
Yea, though I walk through the valley of the
shadow of death, I will fear no evil; for You are
with me; Your rod and Your staff, they comfort me.

You prepare a table before me in the presence
of my enemies; You anoint my head with oil;
my cup runs over.

Surely goodness and mercy shall follow me all
the days of my life; and I will dwell in the house
of the LORD forever.

PSALM 23:1-6 NKJV

*Genuine love sees faces, not a mass:
the Good Shepherd calls
His own sheep by name.*

— *George A. Buttrick* —

91

AS GOOD AS HIS WORD

So shall My word be that goes forth from My mouth; it shall not return to Me void, but it shall accomplish what I please, and it shall prosper in the thing for which I sent it.

ISAIAH 55:11 NKJV

For the word of the LORD holds true, and we can trust everything he does. He loves whatever is just and good; the unfailing love of the LORD fills the earth.

PSALM 33:4-5 NLT

Not one word has failed of all His good promise.

1 KINGS 8:56 NASB

I wait for the LORD...and in his word
I put my hope. My soul waits for the Lord
more than watchmen wait for the morning.

PSALM 130:5-6 NIV

Let the morning bring me word of your
unfailing love, for I have put my trust in you.

PSALM 143:8 NIV

*Trust God where you cannot trace Him.
Do not try to penetrate the cloud He
brings over you; rather look to the bow
that is on it. The mystery is God's;
the promise is yours.*

— *John MacDuff* —

93

MADE PERFECT IN WEAKNESS

The LORD is like a father to his children, tender
and compassionate to those who fear him.
For he knows how weak we are; he remembers
we are only dust. Our days on earth
are like grass; like wildflowers, we bloom
and die. The wind blows, and we are gone—
as though we had never been here.

But the love of the LORD remains forever with
those who fear him. His salvation extends to the
children's children of those who are faithful to
his covenant, of those who
obey his commandments!

The LORD has made the heavens his throne;
from there he rules over everything.

PSALM 103:13-19 NLT

He remembered us in our weakness.
His faithful love endures forever.

PSALM 136:23 NLT

My grace is sufficient for thee: for my strength
is made perfect in weakness.

2 CORINTHIANS 12:9 KJV

*We may not see the shining of the promises—
but they still shine! [His strength] is not for
one moment less because of our human weakness.*

— Amy Carmichael —

Bless the LORD,

O my soul,

and all that is within me,

bless his holy name!

Bless the LORD,

O my soul,

and forget not all his benefits,

who forgives all your iniquity,

who heals all your diseases,

who redeems your life from the pit,

who crowns you with

steadfast love and mercy,

who satisfies you with good

so that your youth is renewed

like the eagle's.

PSALM 103:1-5 ESV

He has remembered his love and his
faithfulness...: all the ends of the earth have
seen the salvation of our God.

PSALM 98:3 NIV

Remember me in the light of your unfailing
love, for you are merciful, O LORD.

PSALM 25:7 NLT

Always new.... Always full of promise.
The mornings of our lives, each a
personal daily miracle!

— Gloria Gaither —

FAITHFUL FROM
EVERY ANGLE

O LORD, our Lord, how majestic is your name
in all the earth! You have set your glory above
the heavens.... When I consider your heavens,
the work of your fingers, the moon and the
stars, which you have set in place, what is man
that you are mindful of him, the son of man that
you care for him? You made him a little lower
than the heavenly beings and crowned him with
glory and honor.... O LORD, our Lord, how
majestic is your name in all the earth!

PSALM 8:1, 3-5, 9 NIV

I will praise you with music on the harp,
because you are faithful to your promises,
O my God.

PSALM 71:22 NLT

Search high and low, scan skies and land,
you'll find nothing and no one quite like GOD.
The holy angels are in awe before him; he looms
immense and august over everyone around him.
GOD-of-the-Angel-Armies, who is like you,
powerful and faithful from every angle?

PSALM 89:6-8 THE MESSAGE

Angels bright,

heavens high,

waters deep,

give God the praise.

— *Christopher Collins* —

DEEP AND HIDDEN THINGS

He gives wisdom to the wise and knowledge
to those who have understanding. He reveals
deep and hidden things; he knows what is in the
darkness, and light dwells with him.

DANIEL 2:21-22 NRSV

My purpose is that they may be encouraged in
heart and united in love, so that they may have
the full riches of complete understanding, in
order that they may know the mystery of God,
namely, Christ, in whom are hidden all the
treasures of wisdom and knowledge.

COLOSSIANS 2:2-3 NIV

The secret things belong unto the LORD our God:
but those things which are revealed belong unto us.

DEUTERONOMY 29:29 KJV

For now we see in a mirror dimly , but then
face to face; now I know in part, but then I will
know fully just as I also have been fully known.

1 CORINTHIANS 13:12 NASB

*We shall come one day to a heaven where
we shall gratefully know that God's great
refusals were sometimes the true answers*

to our truest prayer.

— *P.T. Forsyth* —

OUR GREAT HIGH PRIEST

And God is able to make all grace abound
to you, so that in all things at all times,
having all that you need, you will abound
in every good work.

2 CORINTHIANS 9:8 NIV

Since we have a great high priest
who has passed through the heavens,
Jesus the Son of God,
let us hold fast our confession.
For we do not have a high priest who
cannot sympathize with our weaknesses,
but One who has been tempted
in all things as we are, yet without sin.

Therefore let us draw near with confidence to the throne of grace, so that we may receive mercy and find grace to help in time of need.

HEBREWS 4:14-16 NASB

For there is one God and one mediator between God and men, the man Christ Jesus, who gave himself as a ransom for all men.

1 TIMOTHY 2:5-6 NIV

It is God to whom and with whom we travel, and while He is the End of our journey, He is also at every stopping place.

— *Elisabeth Elliot* —

NEAR TO ALL WHO CALL

On the day I called, You answered me; You
made me bold with strength in my soul....
For great is the glory of the LORD.... Though
I walk in the midst of trouble, You will revive
me; You will stretch forth Your hand...and
Your right hand will save me. The LORD
will accomplish what concerns me; Your
lovingkindness, O LORD, is everlasting; do not
forsake the works of Your hands.

PSALM 138:3, 5, 7-8 NASB

Oh give thanks to the LORD, call upon His
name; make known His deeds among the
peoples.... Seek the Lord and His strength;
seek His face continually.

PSALM 105:1, 4 NASB

The LORD is righteous in all His ways, gracious
in all His works. The LORD is near to all who call
upon Him, to all who call upon Him in truth.
He will fulfill the desire of those who fear Him;
He also will hear their cry and save them.

PSALM 145:17-19 NKJV

*Christ desires to be with you in whatever
crisis you may find yourself. Call upon
His name. See if He will not do as
He promised He would.*

— *Billy Graham* —

Happy are those who do not follow the advice of the wicked, or take the path that sinners tread, or sit in the seat of scoffers; but their delight is in the law of the Lord, and on his law they meditate day and night. They are like trees planted by streams of water, which yield their fruit in its season, and their leaves do not wither.

PSALM 1:1-3 NRSV

Whoever drinks of the water that I will give him shall never thirst; but the water that I will give him will become in him a well of water springing up to eternal life.

JOHN 4:14 NASB

As the deer pants for streams of water,
so my soul pants for you, O God. My soul
thirsts for God, for the living God.

PSALM 42:1-2 NIV

*Drink deeply from the very Source the
deep calm and peace of interior quietude and
refreshment of God, allowing the pure water
of divine grace to flow plentifully and
unceasingly from the Source itself.*

— *Mother Teresa* —

GUARD YOUR HEART

Above all else, guard your heart,
for it is the wellspring of life.

PROVERBS 4:23 NIV

Love the LORD your God with all your heart
and with all your soul and with all your might.
And these words that I command you today
shall be on your heart.

DEUTERONOMY 6:5-6 ESV

Therefore we do not lose heart. Though
outwardly we are wasting away, yet inwardly
we are being renewed day by day.

2 CORINTHIANS 4:16 NIV

My flesh and my heart may fail, but God is the
strength of my heart and my portion forever.

PSALM 73:26 NIV

I will give them an undivided heart
and put a new spirit in them; I will
remove from them their heart of stone
and give them a heart of flesh.

EZEKIEL 11:19 NIV

*In the deepest heart of everyone,
God planted a longing for Himself
as He is: a God of love.*

— *Eugenia Price* —

SEND FORTH YOUR LIGHT

The LORD will guide you always;
he will satisfy your needs in a sun-scorched land.

ISAIAH 58:11 NIV

Delight yourself in the LORD and he will give you
the desires of your heart. Commit your way to
the LORD; trust in him and he will do this: He will
make your righteousness shine like the dawn, the
justice of your cause like the noonday sun.

PSALM 37:4-6 NIV

Send forth your light and your truth,
let them guide me; let them bring me to your
holy mountain, to the place where you dwell.

PSALM 43:3 NIV

Every good gift and every perfect gift is
from above, and cometh down from the
Father of lights, with whom is no variableness,
neither shadow of turning.

JAMES 1:17 KJV

*Infinite wisdom...brings order
out of confusion, and light out of darkness,
and, to those who love God, causes all things...
to work together for good.*

— J. L. Dagg —

MY HELP AND SHIELD

I will lift up my eyes to the hills—
from whence comes my help?
My help comes from the LORD,
who made heaven and earth.
He will not allow your foot to be moved;
He who keeps you will not slumber.
Behold, He who keeps Israel
shall neither slumber nor sleep.
The LORD is your keeper;
the LORD is your shade at your right hand.
The sun shall not strike you by day,
nor the moon by night.
The LORD shall preserve you from all evil;
He shall preserve your soul.
The LORD shall preserve your going out
and your coming in from this time forth,
and even forevermore.

PSALM 121:1-8 NKJV

If you don't know what you're doing,
pray to the Father. He loves to help.

JAMES 1:5 THE MESSAGE

Trust the Lord! He is your helper
and your shield.

PSALM 115:9 NLT

*We have a Father in heaven who
is almighty, who loves His children as
He loves His only-begotten Son,
and whose very joy and delight it is to...help
them at all times and under all circumstances.*

— George Mueller —

AT EVERY MOMENT

Who shall separate us from the love of Christ? Shall trouble or hardship or persecution or famine or nakedness or danger or sword?... No, in all these things we are more than conquerors through him who loved us. For I am convinced that neither death nor life, neither angels nor demons, neither the present nor the future, nor any powers, neither height nor depth, nor anything else in all creation, will be able to separate us from the love of God that is in Christ Jesus our Lord.

ROMANS 8:35, 37-39 NIV

The LORD will work out his plans for my life — for your faithful love, O LORD, endures forever.

PSALM 138:8 NLT

Show Your marvelous lovingkindness by Your right hand, O You who save those who trust in You.... Keep me as the apple of Your eye; hide me under the shadow of Your wings.

PSALM 17:7-8 NKJV

Let your faith in Christ, the omnipresent One, be in the quiet confidence that He will every day and every moment keep you as the apple of His eye, keep you in perfect peace.

— Andrew Murray —

A TOWER OF STRENGTH

Hear my cry, O God; give heed to my prayer.
From the end of the earth I call to You when
my heart is faint; lead me to the rock that is
higher than I. For You have been a refuge for
me, a tower of strength against the enemy.
Let me dwell in Your tent forever;
let me take refuge in the shelter of Your wings.

PSALM 61:1-4 NASB

You are my strength; I wait for you to rescue
me, for you, O God, are my fortress. In his
unfailing love, my God will stand with me.

PSALM 59:9-10 NLT

The joy of the LORD is your strength.

NEHEMIAH 8:10 KJV

In returning and rest shall ye be saved;

in quietness and in confidence

shall be your strength.

ISAIAH 30:15 KJV

The LORD is my strength and my shield;

my heart trusted in him, and I am helped.

PSALM 28:7 KJV

God's love is like a river springing up in the Divine Substance and flowing endlessly through His creation, filling all things with life and goodness and strength.

— *Thomas Merton* —

MADE WHOLE

May God himself, the God who makes
everything holy and whole, make you holy
and whole, put you together—spirit, soul, and
body—and keep you fit for the coming of our
Master, Jesus Christ. The One who called you
is completely dependable.

1 THESSALONIANS 5:23-24 THE MESSAGE

This we also pray for, that you be made
complete.... Finally, brethren, rejoice,
be made complete, be comforted,
be like-minded, live in peace; and the God
of love and peace will be with you.

2 CORINTHIANS 13:9, 11 NASB

GOD COMFORTS YOU { A Treasury of God's Promises }

Long before he laid down earth's foundations,
he had us in mind, had settled on us as
the focus of his love, to be made whole
and holy by his love.

EPHESIANS 1:4 THE MESSAGE

And we know that all things work together
for good to those who love God.

ROMANS 8:28 NKJV

The mystery of life is that the Lord of life cannot be known except in and through the act of living.... Therefore, we are called each day to present to our Lord the whole of our lives.

— Henri J. M. Nouwen —

119

HIS NAME AND RENOWN

The LORD is a shelter for the oppressed,
a refuge in times of trouble. Those who know
your name trust in you, for you, O LORD, do not
abandon those who search for you. Sing praises
to the LORD who reigns.... Tell the world about
his unforgettable deeds.... He does not ignore
the cries of those who suffer.

PSALM 9:9-12 NLT

For you have exalted above all things
your name and your word.

PSALM 138:2 NIV

Our help is in the name of the LORD,
who made heaven and earth.

PSALM 124:8 KJV

Not to us, O LORD, not to us, but to Your name
give glory because of Your lovingkindness,
because of Your truth.

PSALM 115:1 NASB

Yes, LORD, walking in the way of your laws,
we wait for you; your name and renown are the
desire of our hearts.

ISAIAH 26:8 NIV

*By this name, God announced Himself as the
"great I AM"—the One who is completely and
consistently Himself.... And it is because He
is what He is that everything else is as it is.*

— J. I. Packer —

FAITHFUL PROMISES

Let us draw near to God.... Let us hold
unswervingly to the hope we profess,
for he who promised is faithful.

HEBREWS 10:22-23 NIV

Remember your promise to me; it is my only
hope. Your promise revives me; it comforts me
in all my troubles.... I meditate on your age-old
regulations; O LORD, they comfort me....
Your decrees have been the theme of my songs
wherever I have lived. I reflect at night on who
you are, O LORD; therefore, I obey
your instructions....
Your eternal word, O LORD, stands firm in
heaven. Your faithfulness extends to every
generation, as enduring as the earth
you created.

PSALM 119:49-50, 52, 54-55, 89-90 NLT

I have suffered much, O LORD;
restore my life again as you promised.

PSALM 119:107 NLT

God promises to love me all day, sing songs all
through the night! My life is God's prayer.

PSALM 42:8 THE MESSAGE

Swim through your troubles. Run to
the promises, they are our Lord's branches
hanging over the water so that His children
may take a grip of them.

— *Samuel Rutherford* —

SHOWERS IN SEASON

I will bless my people.... And in the proper
season I will send the showers they need.
There will be showers of blessing.

EZEKIEL 34:26 NLT

He has not left himself without testimony:
He has shown kindness by giving you rain
from heaven and crops in their seasons;
he provides you with plenty of food
and fills your hearts with joy.

ACTS 14:17-18 NIV

Rejoice in the LORD your God! For the rain he
sends demonstrates his faithfulness.

JOEL 2:23 NLT

For, lo, the winter is past, the rain is over and gone; the flowers appear on the earth; the time of the singing of birds is come.

SONG OF SOLOMON 2:11-12 KJV

So let us know, let us press on to know the LORD.... He will come to us like the rain, like the spring rain watering the earth.

HOSEA 6:3 NASB

God is the sunshine that warms us, the rain that melts the frost and waters the young plants. The presence of God is a climate of strong and bracing love, always there.

— *Joan Arnold* —

BE STILL AND KNOW

Let those who boast boast in this, that they
understand and know me, that I am the
Lord; I act with steadfast love, justice, and
righteousness in the earth, for in these things
I delight, says the Lord.

JEREMIAH 9:24 NRSV

Be still, and know that I am God.

PSALM 46:10 KJV

He calls his own sheep by name and leads them
out.... His sheep follow him because they know
his voice.

JOHN 10:3-4 NIV

I will betroth you to Me in righteousness and
in justice, in lovingkindness and in compassion,
and I will betroth you to Me in faithfulness.
Then you will know the LORD.

HOSEA 2:19-20 NASB

That I may know him, and the power
of his resurrection, and the fellowship
of his sufferings.

PHILIPPIANS 3:10 KJV

*In our unquenchable longing to
know God personally, we pursue
Him with passion and find He is
relentless in His pursuit of us.*

EVERLASTING LOVE

I have loved you with an
everlasting love; I have drawn you
with loving-kindness.

JEREMIAH 31:3 NIV